PLAY IT
LIKE IT IS
GUITAR
WITH TABLATURE

NOTE-FOR-NOTE
TRANSCRIPTIONS

HERE'S THE
SeX PisTOLs

NEVER MIND
THE BOLLOCKS

This book was approved by the Sex Pistols

ISBN-13: 978-1-57560-943-0
ISBN-10: 1-57560-943-6

Visit our website at www.cherrylane.com

HERE'S THE SeX PiSTOLs

HOLIDAYS IN THE SUN

Words and Music by
Paul Thomas Cook, Stephen Philip Jones,
John Simon Beverly and John Lydon

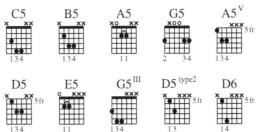

11

Bridge

star - ing all night, and they're star - ing all day. I _____ had no rea - son to be here at all. _____ But now I got a rea - son. It's no real _____ rea - son, and I'm wait - ing. _____ The Ber - lin _____ wall. _____ I got - ta go o - ver the Ber - lin

13

Coda

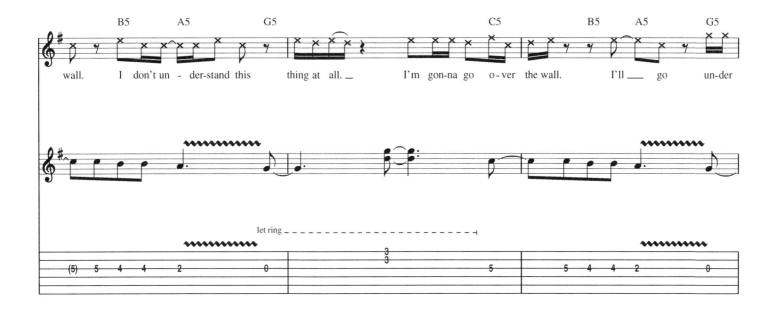

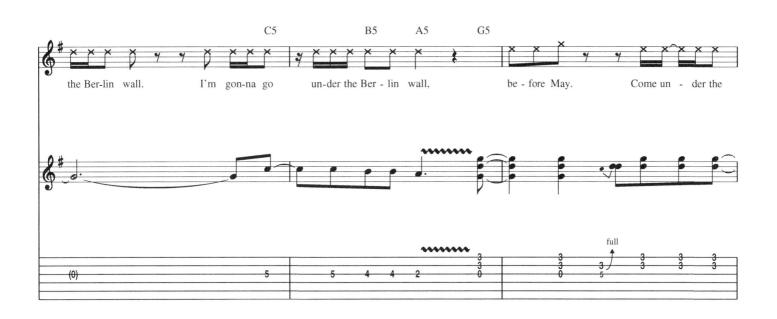

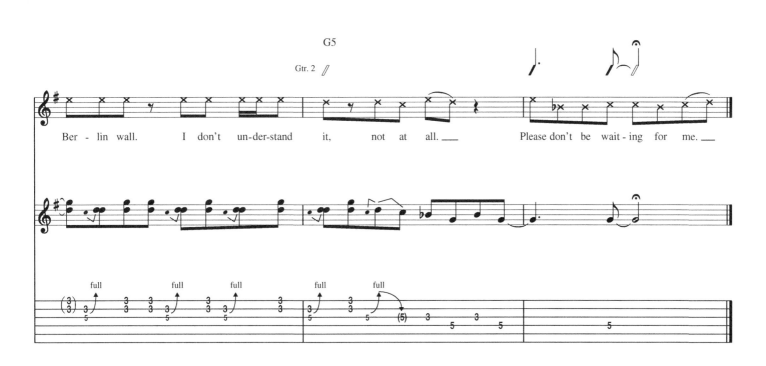

15

BODIES

Words and Music by
Paul Thomas Cook, Stephen Philip Jones,
John Simon Beverly and John Lydon

17

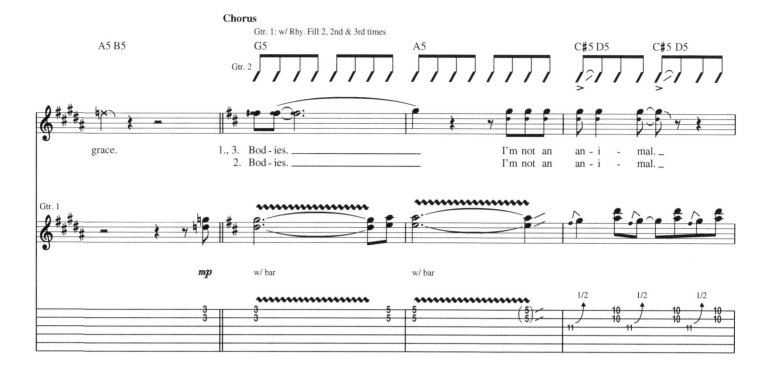

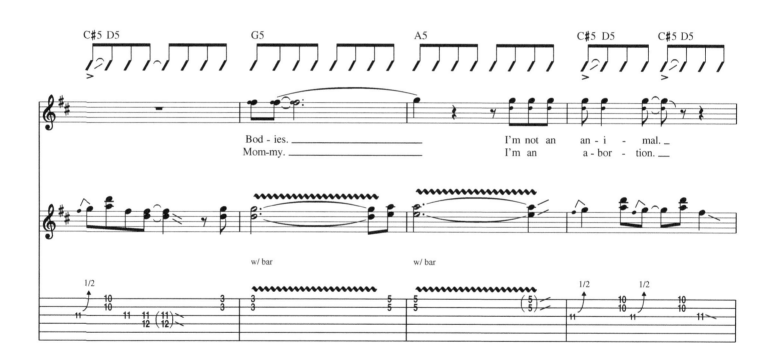

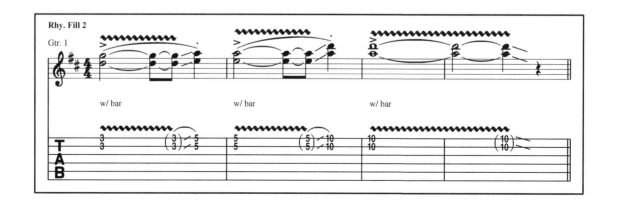

19

NO FEELINGS

Words and Music by
Paul Thomas Cook, Stephen Philip Jones,
Glen Matlock and John Lydon

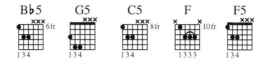

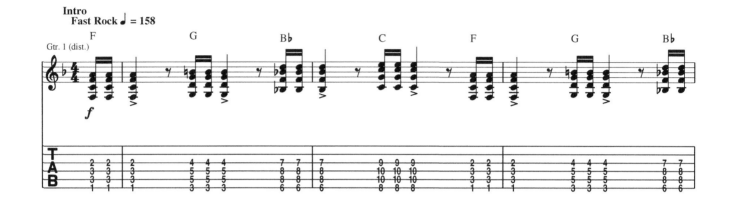

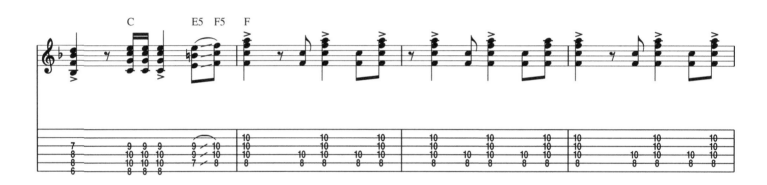

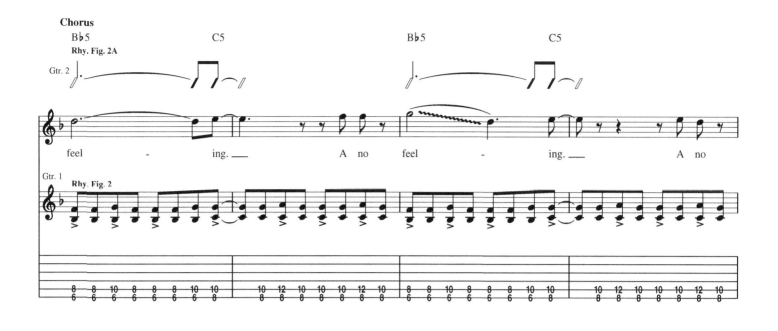

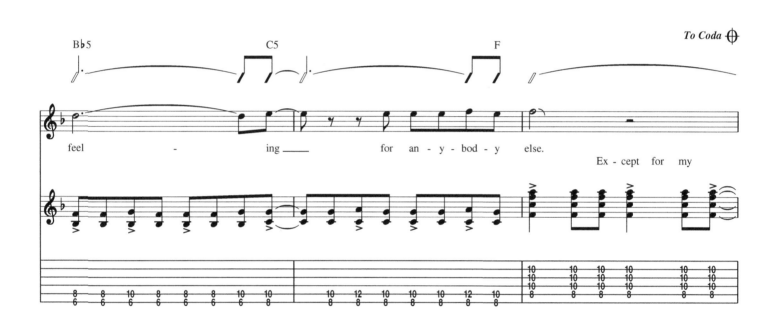

Guitar Solo

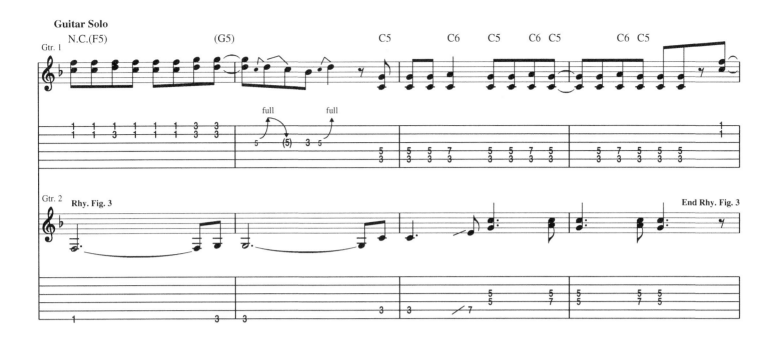

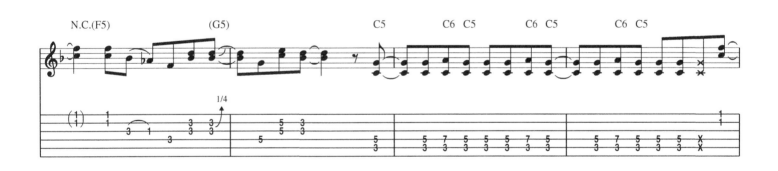

D.S. al Coda

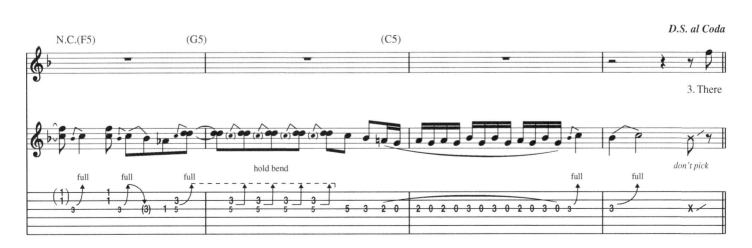

3. There

⊕ Coda

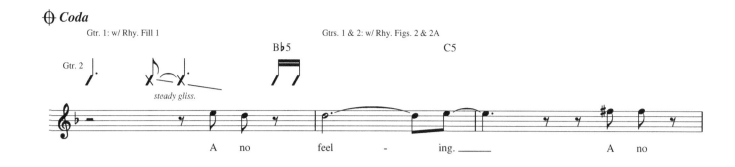

A no feel - ing. _____ A no

feel - ing. _____ A no feel - ing ____

____ for an - y - bod - y else, ex - cept for my - self. Your dad - dy's gone a -

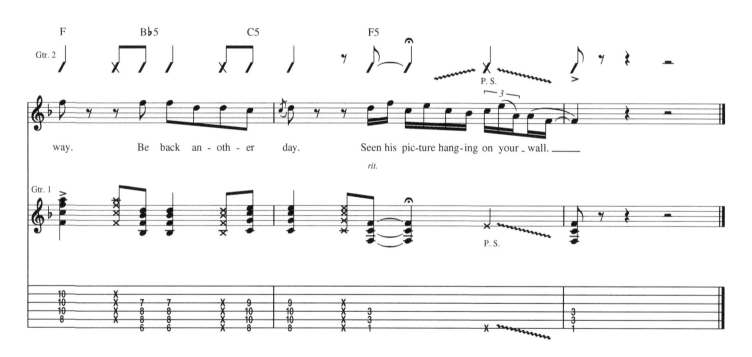

way. Be back an - oth - er day. Seen his pic - ture hang - ing on your _ wall. _____

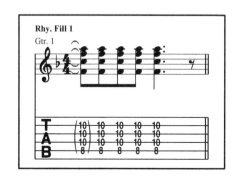

LIAR

Words and Music by
Paul Thomas Cook, Stephen Philip Jones,
Glen Matlock and John Lydon

26

do or say. _____ So when you tell lies _____ I'll al - ways
You're _____

be in your way. _____ I'm no - bod - y's fool, and I _____ know ___ all. Cause I
___ in sus - pen - sion. _____ You're a

*(Gtr. 1 cont. in notation)

*2nd time

Guitar Solo

li - ar. You're a li - ar. _____

End Rhy. Fig. 1

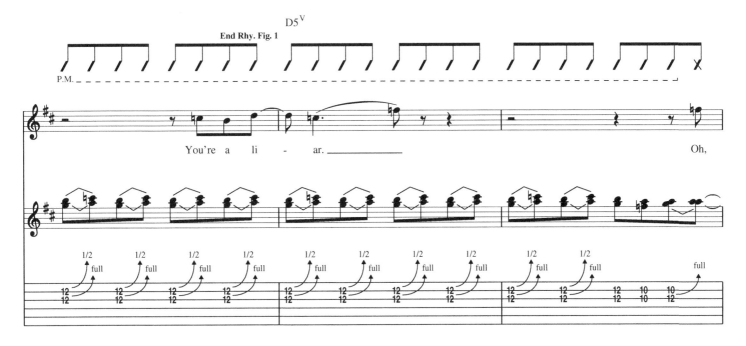

You're a li - ar. _____ Oh,

PROBLEMS

Words and Music by
Paul Thomas Cook, Stephen Philip Jones,
Glen Matlock and John Lydon

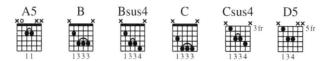

* Key signature denotes A Dorian.

** Chord symbols reflect overall tonality.

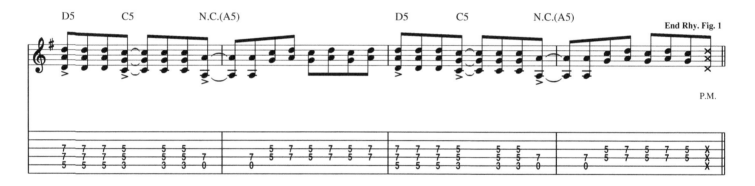

1. Too man-y prob-lems. Oh, why am I here? I need to be me, 'cause you're

2. Eat your heart out on a plas-tic tray. You don't do what you want then you'll

simile on repeats

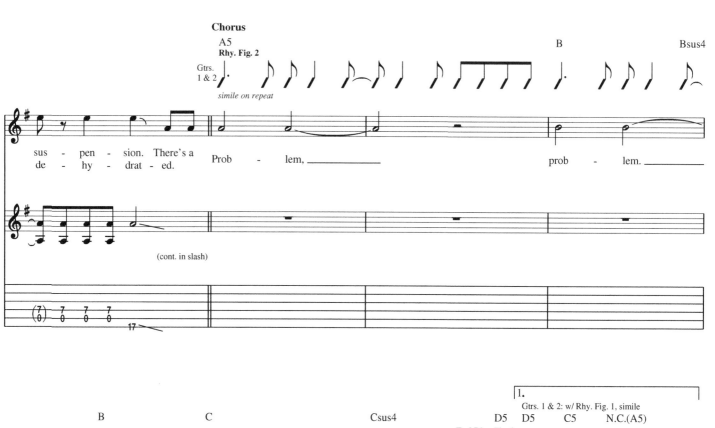

sus - pen - sion. There's a Prob - lem, _____ prob - lem. _____

de - hy - drat - ed.

(cont. in slash)

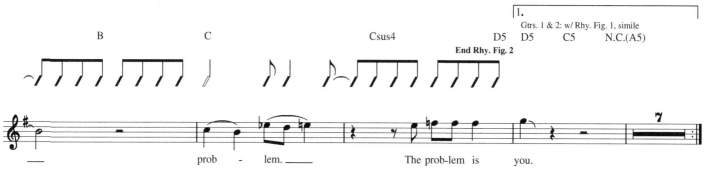

_____ prob - lem. _____ The prob-lem is you.

you. Aw, what you gon - na do? Prob - lem. __

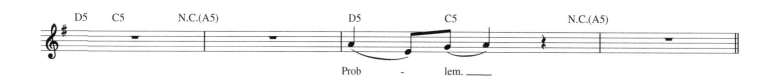

Prob - lem. _____

Guitar Solo

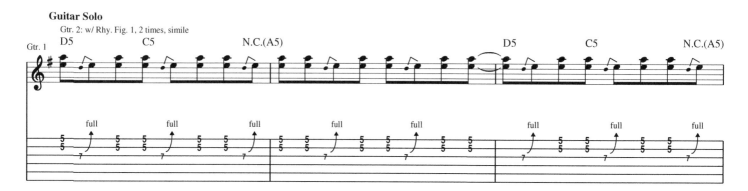

✠ Chorus

Gtr. 1: w/ Rhy. Fig. 2, 1st 4 meas.
Gtr. 2: w/ Rhy. Fig. 2

Gtr. 1: w/ Rhy. Fill 1

Prob - lem, _____ prob - lem, _____ prob - lem. _____

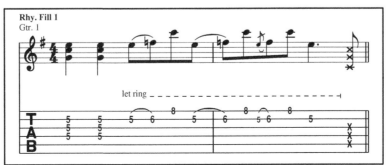

Rhy. Fill 1
Gtr. 1

let ring

all worked out. Bet you thought _ you knew what I was a - bout. _

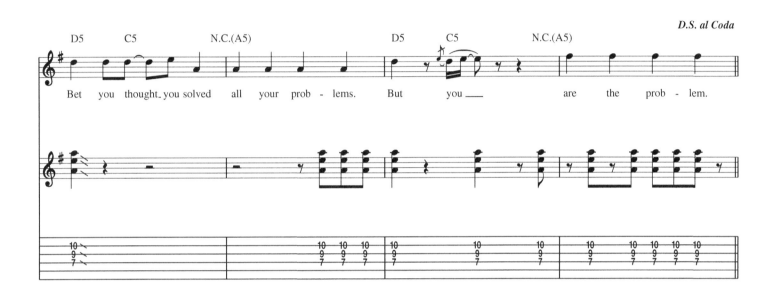

D.S. al Coda

Bet you thought _ you solved all your prob - lems. But you ___ are the prob - lem.

Coda

Gtrs. 1 & 2: w/ Rhy. Fig. 1, simile

you. Aw, what you gon - na do with your prob - lem? ___ I'll

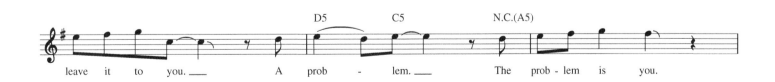

leave it to you. ___ A prob - lem. ___ The prob - lem is you.

Outro

Gtrs. 1 & 2: w/ Rhy. Fig. 1, simile

You got - ta prob - lem? Aw, what you gon - na do?

1. They know a doc - tor gon - na
   don't want you ___ and they
3. Prob - lem, ___ oh
4. Prob - lem, ___ oh

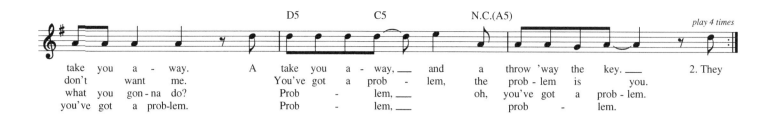

take you a - way.
don't want me.
what you gon - na do?
you've got a prob-lem.

A take you a - way, ___ and a throw 'way the key. ___ 2. They
You've got a prob - lem, the prob - lem is you.
Prob - lem, ___ oh, you've got a prob - lem.
Prob - lem, ___ prob - lem.

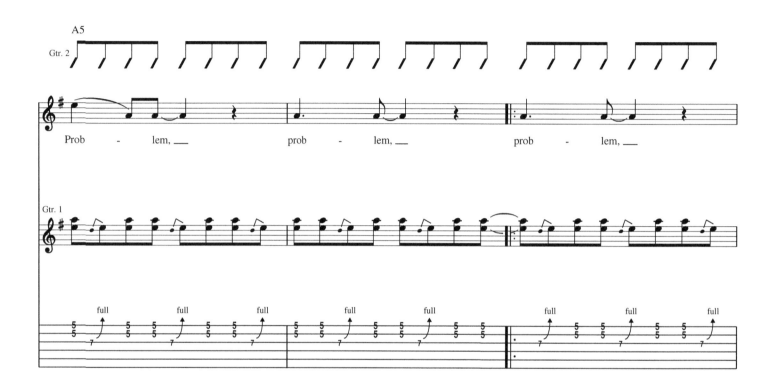

Prob - lem, ___ prob - lem, ___ prob - lem, ___

prob - lem, _ prob - lem, _ prob - lem. _ *Spoken: Problem, problem, problem.*

GOD SAVE THE QUEEN

Words and Music by
Paul Thomas Cook, Stephen Philip Jones,
Glen Matlock and John Lydon

what you need.. There's no fu - ture, no fu - ture, no ___ fu - ture for
dust - bin. __ We're the poi - son in your hu - man ma - chine. We're the fu - ture.

you. __ Your fu - ture. God save the queen. ___ We mean it man.

1., 2. We love our queen. ___ God saves. ____
3. There is no fu - ture, and Eng - land's __

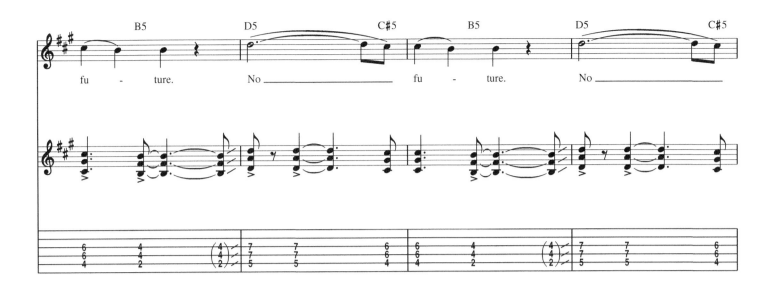

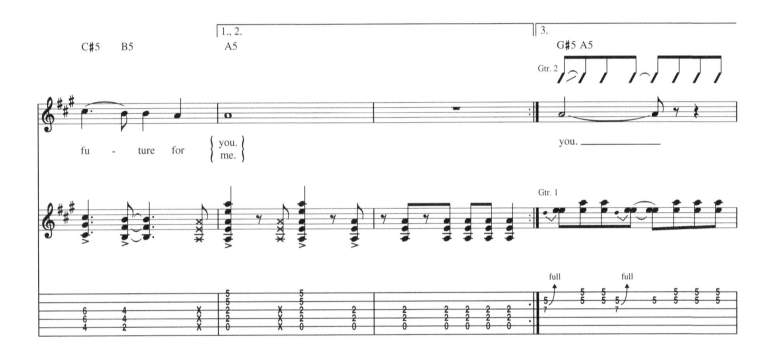

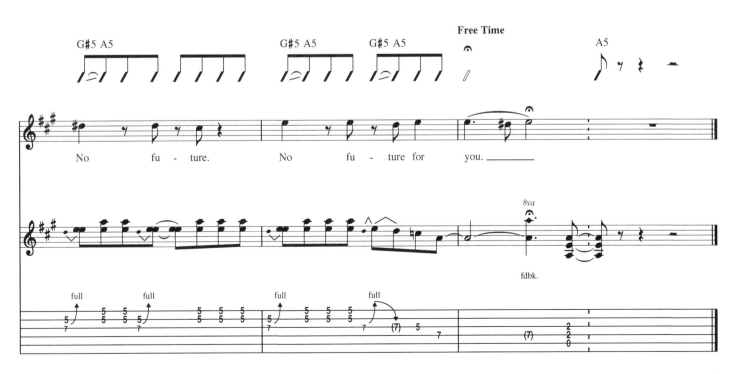

SEVENTEEN

Words and Music by
Paul Thomas Cook, Stephen Philip Jones,
Glen Matlock and John Lydon

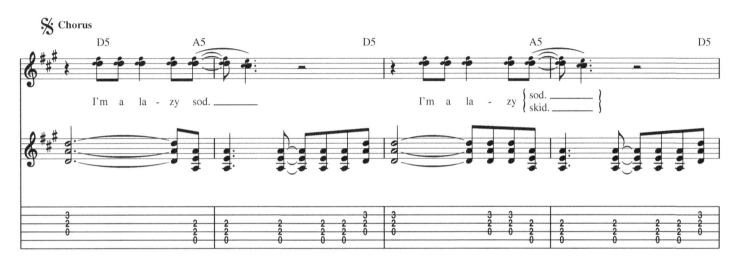

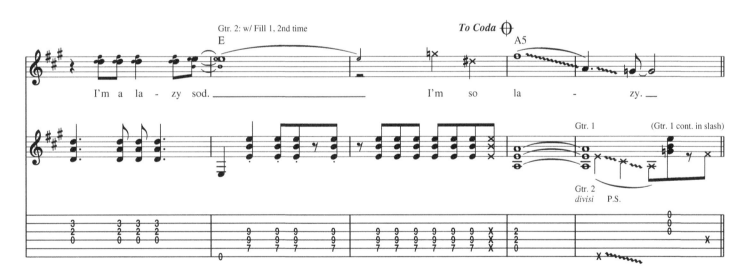

Interlude

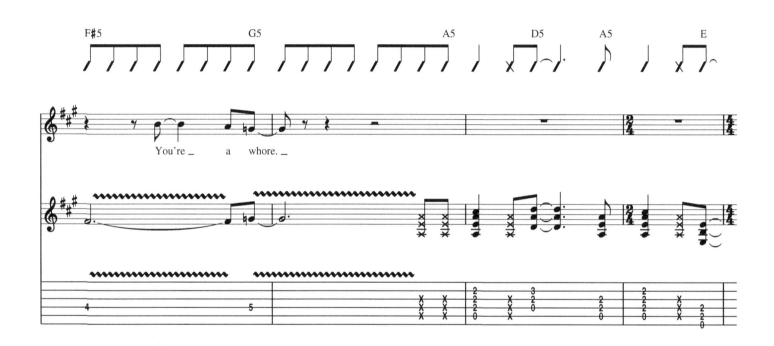

You're _ a whore. _

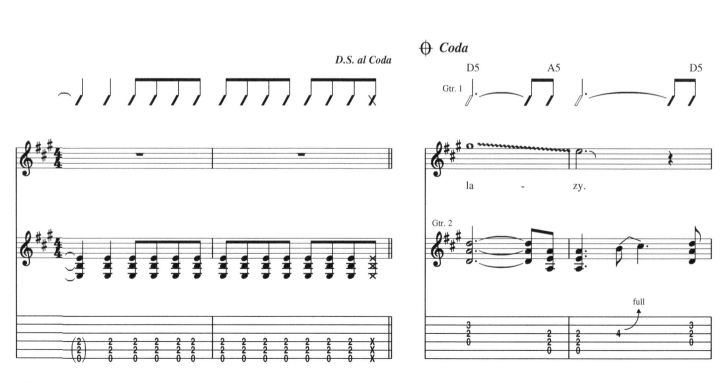

la - zy.

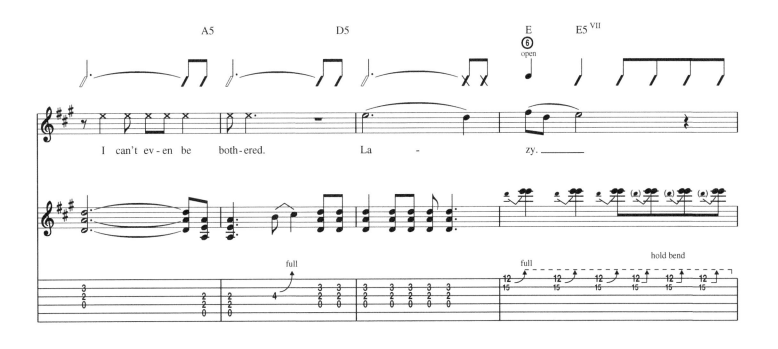

I can't ev-en be both-ered. La - zy. ___

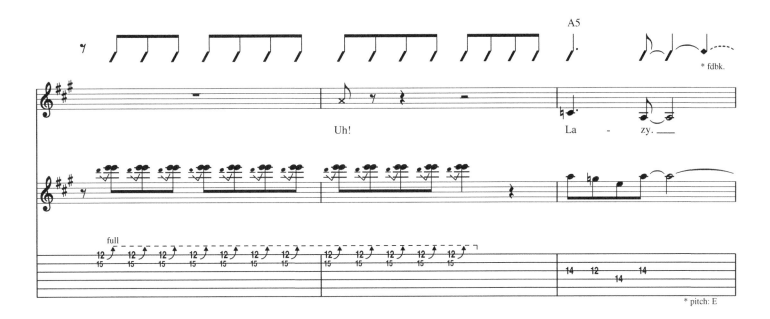

Uh! La - zy. ___

* pitch: E

Free Time

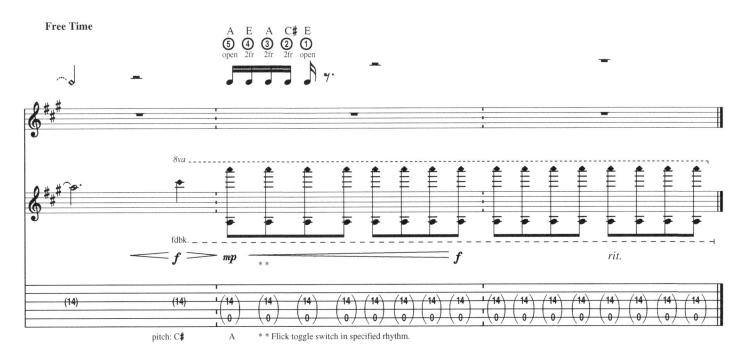

pitch: C#   A   ** Flick toggle switch in specified rhythm.

ANARCHY IN THE U.K.

Words and Music by
Paul Thomas Cook, Stephen Philip Jones,
Glen Matlock and John Lydon

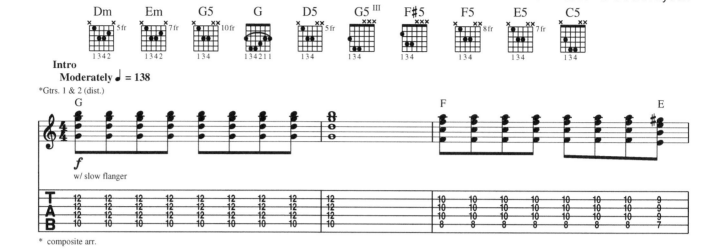

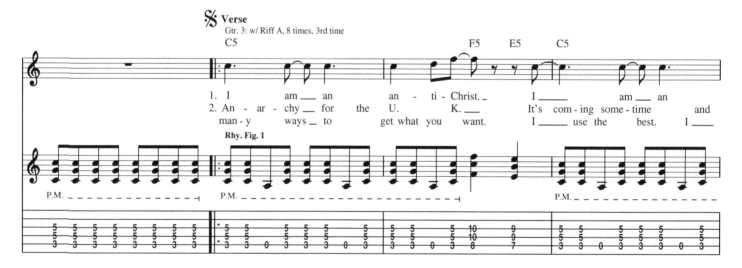

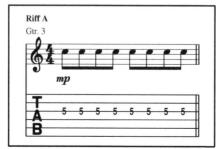

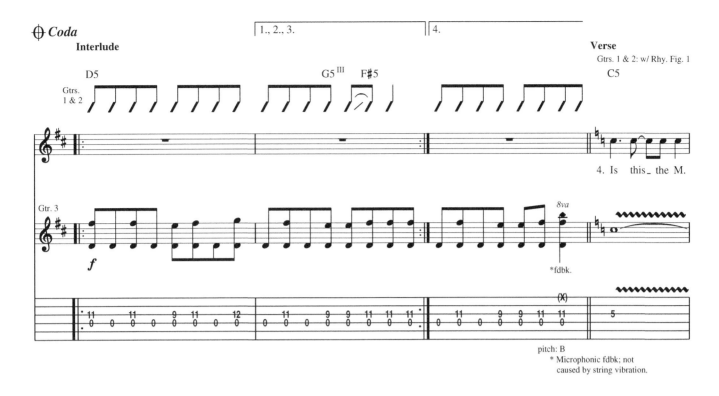

pitch: B
* Microphonic fdbk; not
  caused by string vibration.

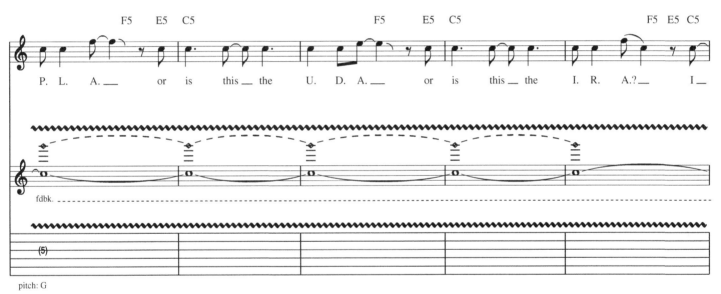

pitch: G

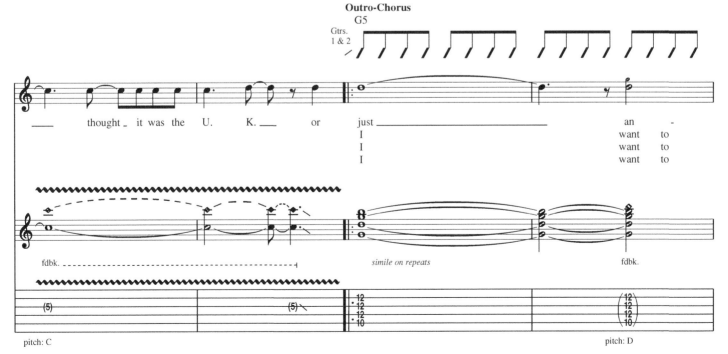

pitch: C

pitch: D

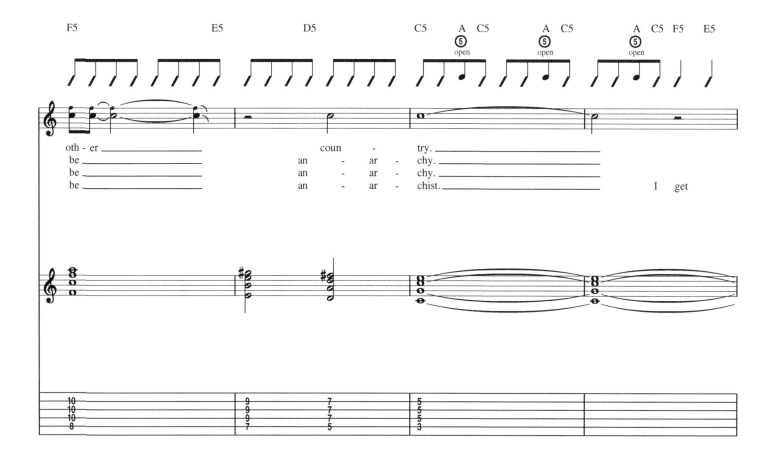

oth - er _____ coun - try. _____
be _____ an - ar - chy. _____
be _____ an - ar - chy. _____
be _____ an - ar - chist. _____ I get

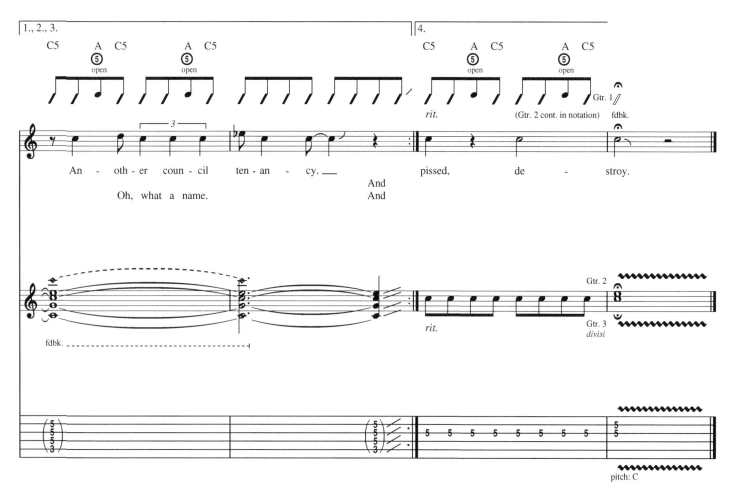

An - oth- er coun - cil ten - an - cy. ___ pissed, de - stroy.
And
Oh, what a name. And

SUBMISSION

Words and Music by
Paul Thomas Cook, Stephen Philip Jones,
Glen Matlock and John Lydon

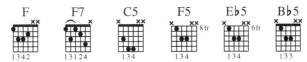

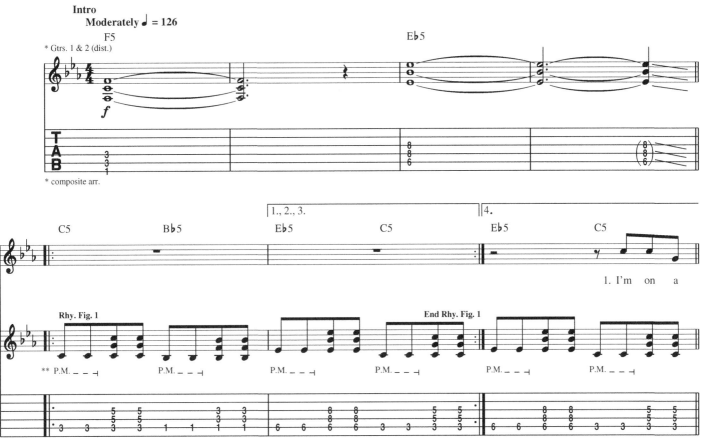

** 3rd gtr. randomly flicks toggle knob next 8 meas.
(lead pickup at 10, rhythm pickup at 0, sounding pitch is C)

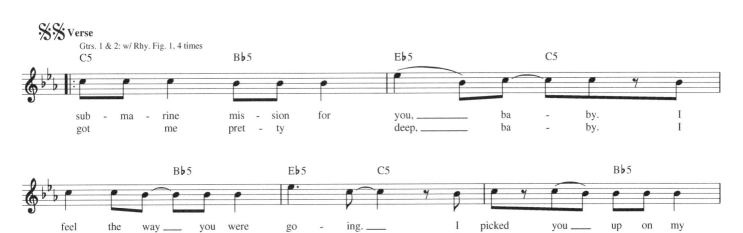

Chorus

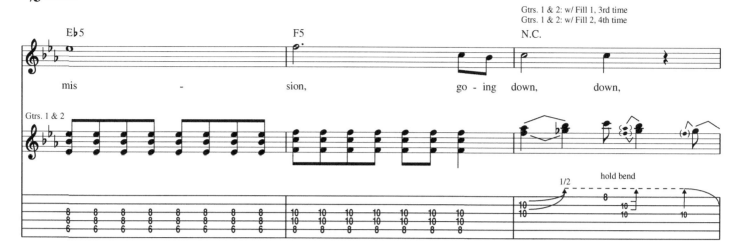

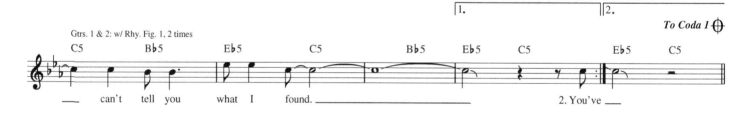

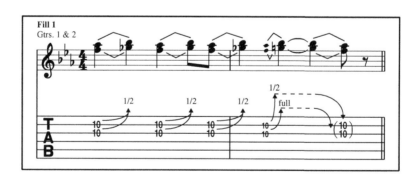

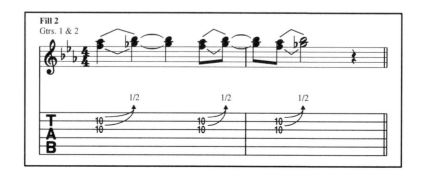

PRETTY VACANT

Words and Music by
Paul Thomas Cook, Stephen Philip Jones,
Glen Matlock and John Lydon

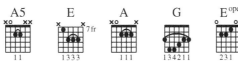

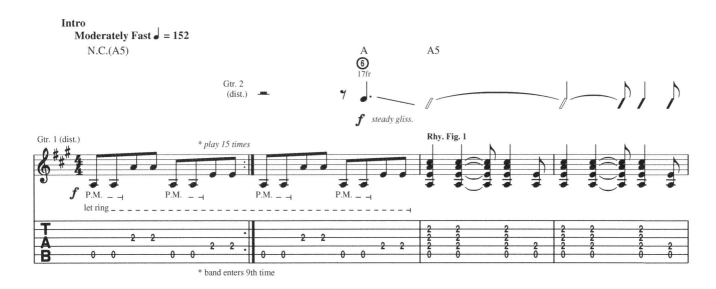

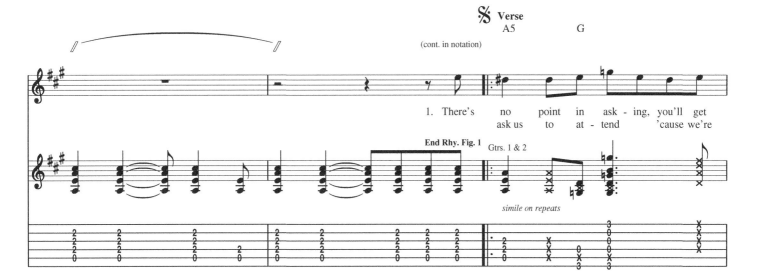

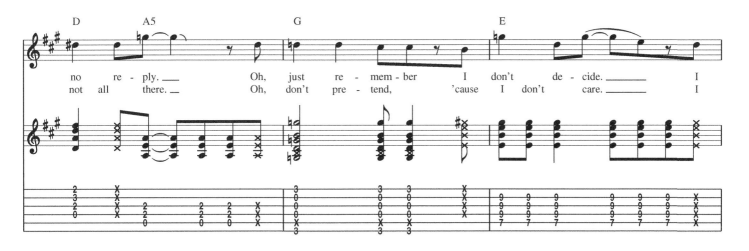

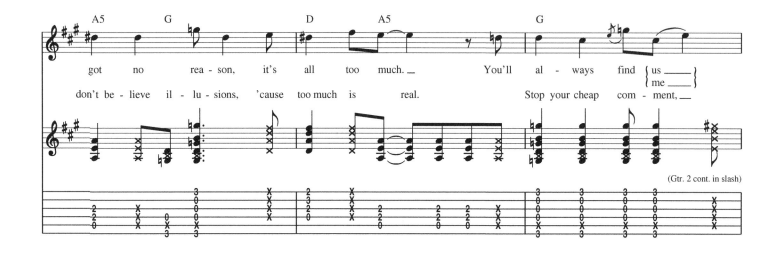

got no rea - son, it's all too much. ___ You'll al - ways find { us ___ }
don't be - lieve il - lu - sions, 'cause too much is real. Stop your cheap com - ment, ___

(Gtr. 2 cont. in slash)

Gtr. 1: w/ Fill 1, 2nd time
Gtr. 1: w/ Fill 2, 3rd time

(cont. in notation)

out to ___ lunch. ___ }
'cause we know what we feel. ___ }

Oh,

Fill 1

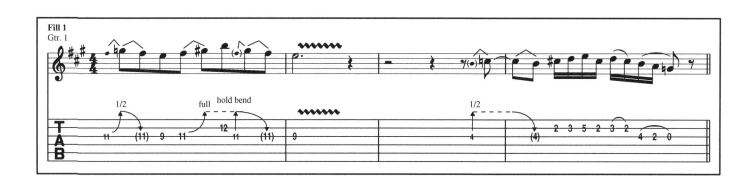

Fill 2

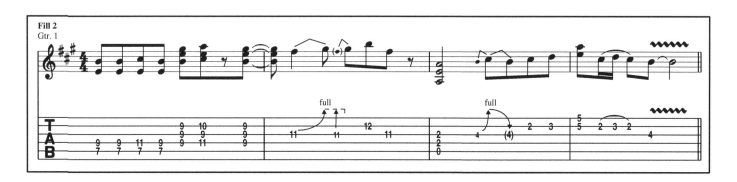

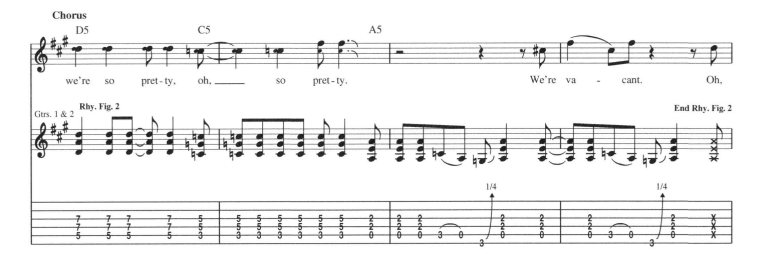

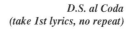

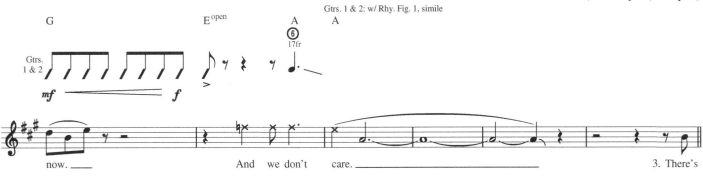

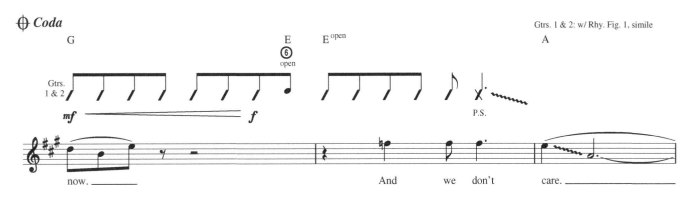

We're pret - ty. _____

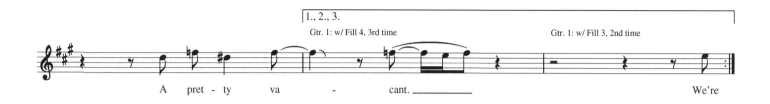

A pret - ty va - cant. _____ We're

- cant, and we don't care. _____

Gtrs. 1 & 2

fdbk. - - - - - -|

Fill 3
Gtr. 1

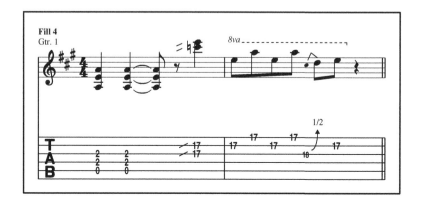

Fill 4
Gtr. 1

NEW YORK

Words and Music by
Paul Thomas Cook, Stephen Philip Jones,
Glen Matlock and John Lydon

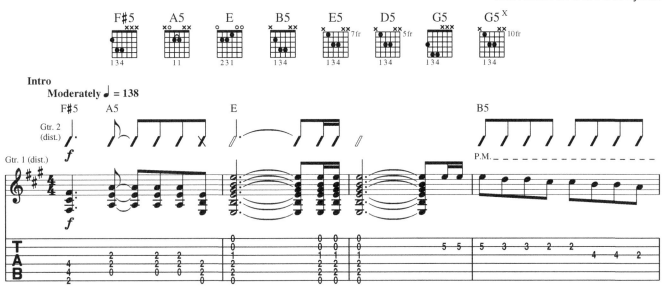

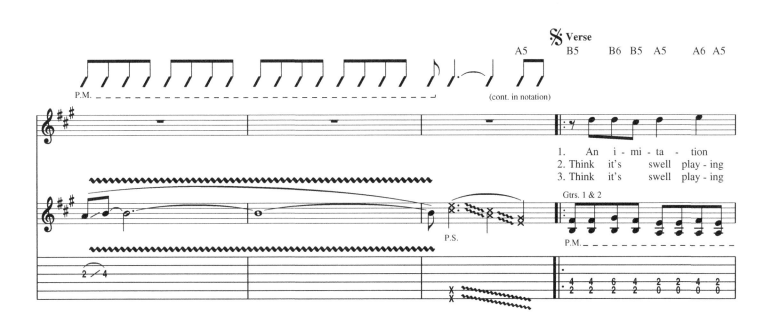

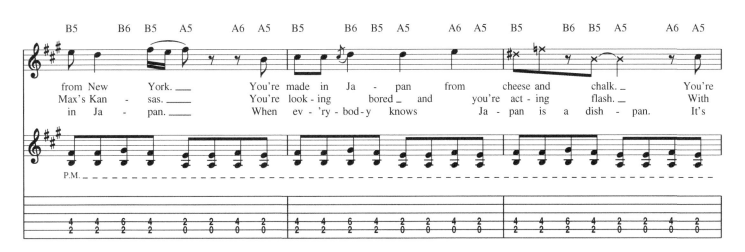

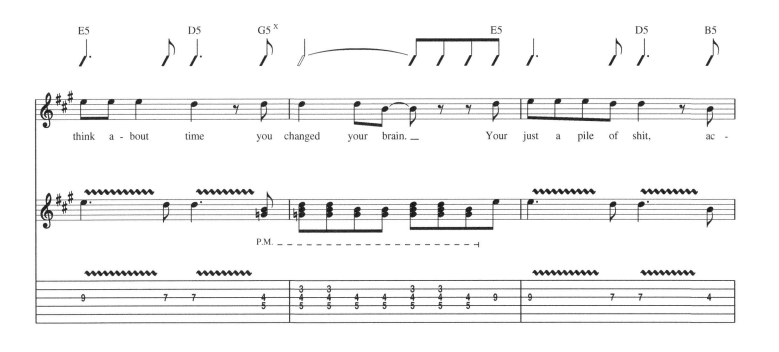

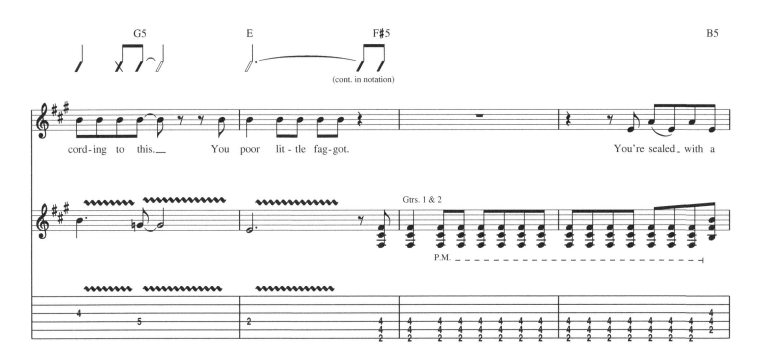

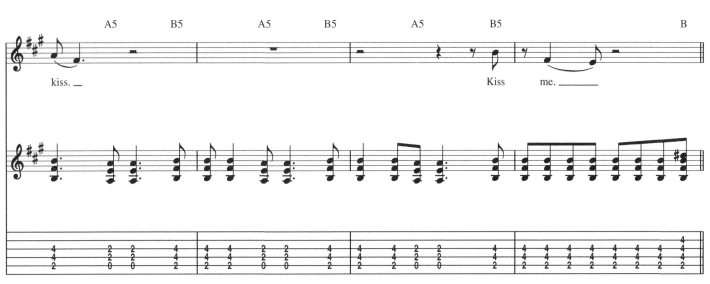

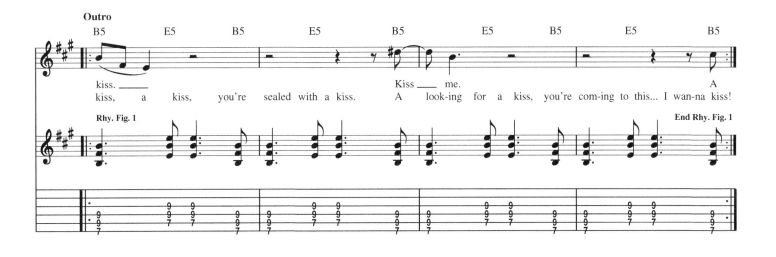

kiss. _____   Kiss _____ me.   A

kiss,   a   kiss,   you're   sealed   with   a   kiss.   A   look-ing   for   a   kiss,   you're   com-ing   to   this...   I   wan-na   kiss!

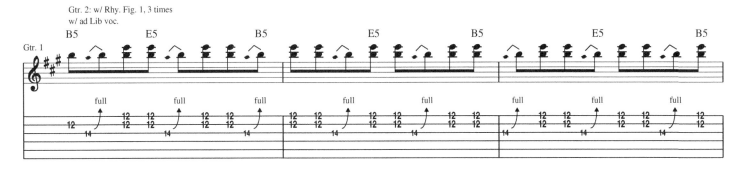

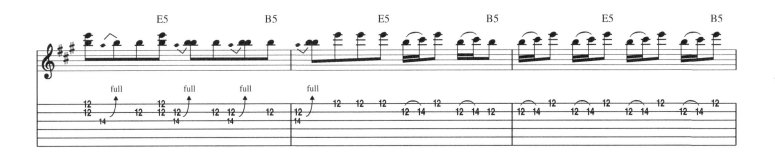

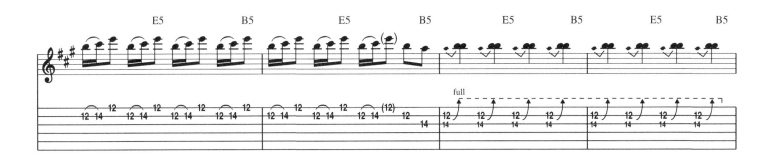

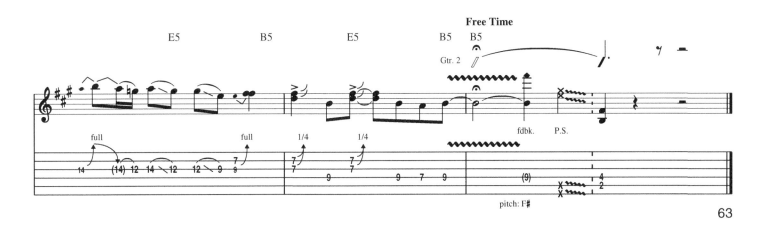

E.M.I.

Words and Music by
Paul Thomas Cook, Stephen Philip Jones,
Glen Matlock and John Lydon

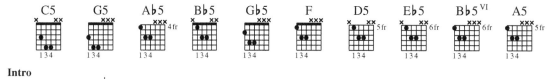

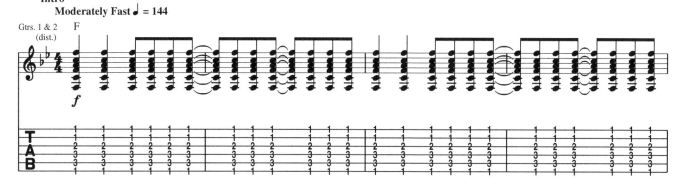

Intro
Moderately Fast ♩ = 144

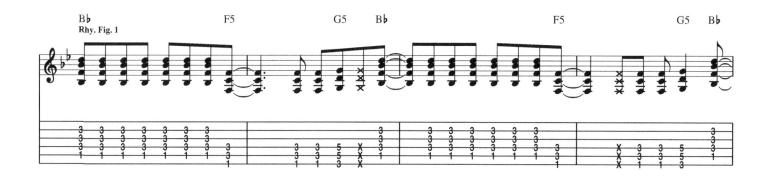

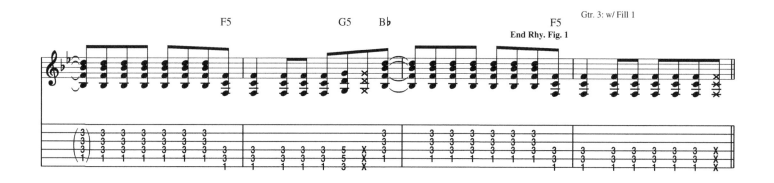

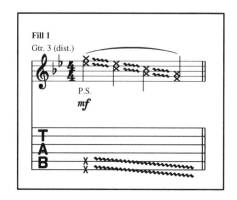

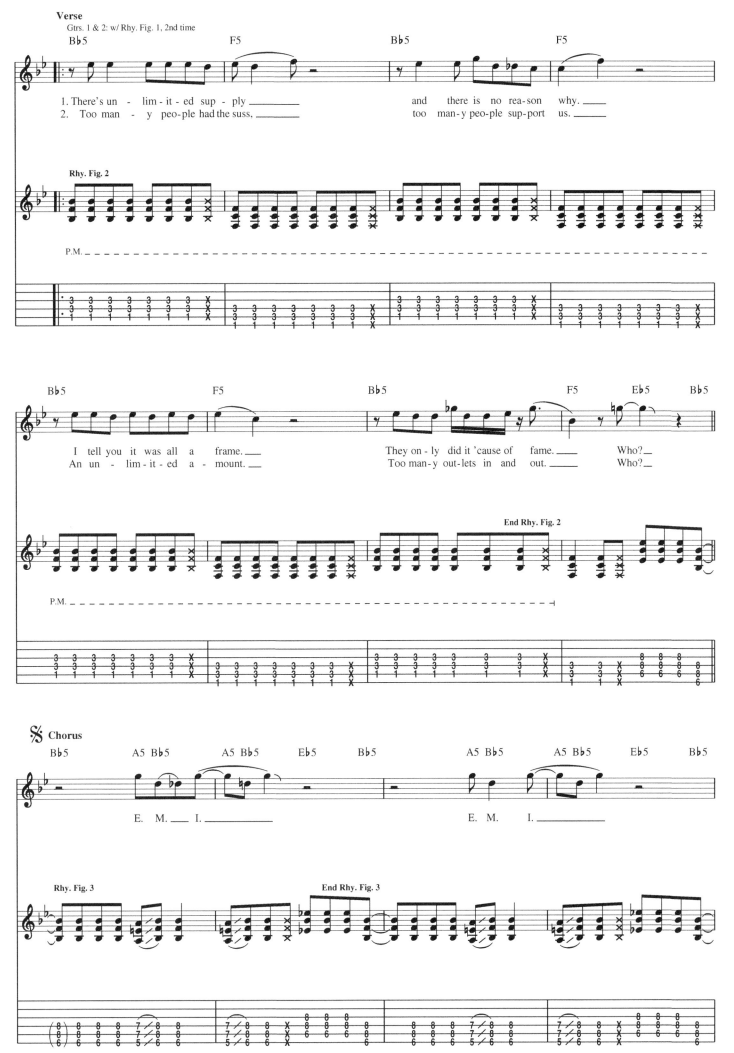

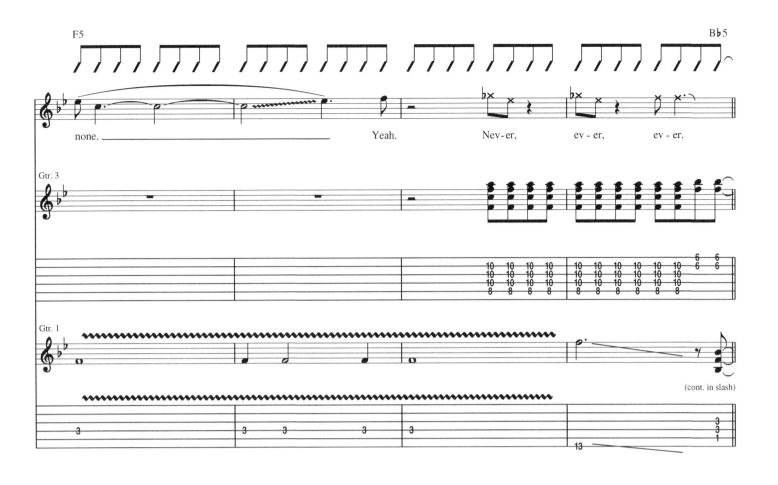

none. _____ Yeah. Nev-er, ev - er, ev - er.

Guitar Solo

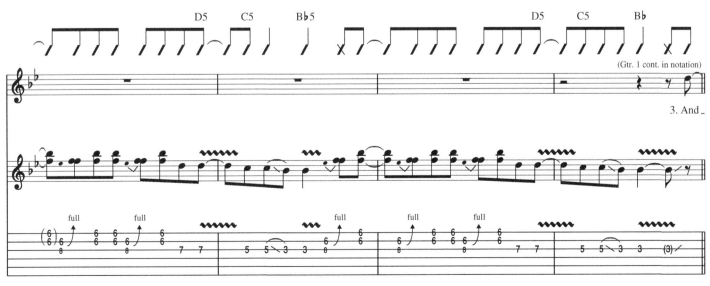

3. And _

Guitar Notation Legend

Guitar Music can be notated three different ways: on a *musical staff*, in *tablature*, and in *rhythm slashes*.

RHYTHM SLASHES are written above the staff. Strum chords in the rhythm indicated. Use the chord diagrams found at the top of the first page of the transcription for the appropriate chord voicings. Round noteheads indicate single notes.

THE MUSICAL STAFF shows pitches and rhythms and is divided by bar lines into measures. Pitches are named after the first seven letters of the alphabet.

TABLATURE graphically represents the guitar fingerboard. Each horizontal line represents a a string, and each number represents a fret.

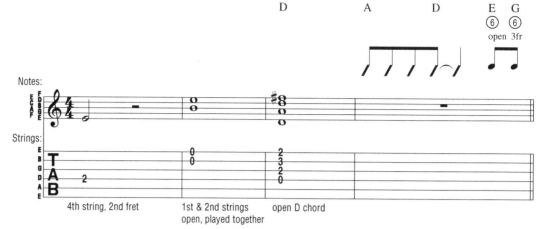

4th string, 2nd fret

1st & 2nd strings open, played together

open D chord

Definitions for Special Guitar Notation

HALF-STEP BEND: Strike the note and bend up 1/2 step.

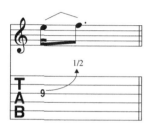

WHOLE-STEP BEND: Strike the note and bend up one step.

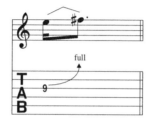

GRACE NOTE BEND: Strike the note and bend up as indicated. The first note does not take up any time.

SLIGHT (MICROTONE) BEND: Strike the note and bend up 1/4 step.

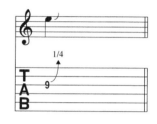

BEND AND RELEASE: Strike the note and bend up as indicated, then release back to the original note. Only the first note is struck.

PRE-BEND: Bend the note as indicated, then strike it.

PRE-BEND AND RELEASE: Bend the note as indicated. Strike it and release the bend back to the original note.

UNISON BEND: Strike the two notes simultaneously and bend the lower note up to the pitch of the higher.

VIBRATO: The string is vibrated by rapidly bending and releasing the note with the fretting hand.

WIDE VIBRATO: The pitch is varied to a greater degree by vibrating with the fretting hand.

HAMMER-ON: Strike the first (lower) note with one finger, then sound the higher note (on the same string) with another finger by fretting it without picking.

PULL-OFF: Place both fingers on the notes to be sounded. Strike the first note and without picking, pull the finger off to sound the second (lower) note.

LEGATO SLIDE: Strike the first note and then slide the same fret-hand finger up or down to the second note. The second note is not struck.

SHIFT SLIDE: Same as legato slide, except the second note is struck.

TRILL: Very rapidly alternate between the notes indicated by continuously hammering on and pulling off.

TAPPING: Hammer ("tap") the fret indicated with the pick-hand index or middle finger and pull off to the note fretted by the fret hand.

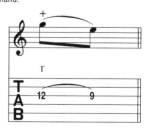

NATURAL HARMONIC: Strike the note while the fret-hand lightly touches the string directly over the fret indicated.

PINCH HARMONIC: The note is fretted normally and a harmonic is produced by adding the edge of the thumb or the tip of the index finger of the pick hand to the normal pick attack.

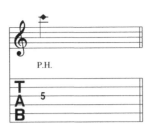

HARP HARMONIC: The note is fretted normally and a harmonic is produced by gently resting the pick hand's index finger directly above the indicated fret (in parentheses) while the pick hand's thumb or pick assists by plucking the appropriate string.

PICK SCRAPE: The edge of the pick is rubbed down (or up) the string, producing a scratchy sound.

MUFFLED STRINGS: A percussive sound is produced by laying the fret hand across the string(s) without depressing, and striking them with the pick hand.

PALM MUTING: The note is partially muted by the pick hand lightly touching the string(s) just before the bridge.

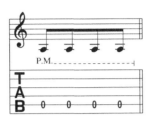

RAKE: Drag the pick across the strings indicated with a single motion.

TREMOLO PICKING: The note is picked as rapidly and continuously as possible.

ARPEGGIATE: Play the notes of the chord indicated by quickly rolling them from bottom to top.

VIBRATO BAR DIVE AND RETURN: The pitch of the note or chord is dropped a specified number of steps (in rhythm) then returned to the original pitch.

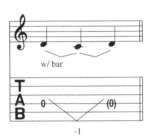

VIBRATO BAR SCOOP: Depress the bar just before striking the note, then quickly release the bar.

VIBRATO BAR DIP: Strike the note and then immediately drop a specified number of steps, then release back to the original pitch.

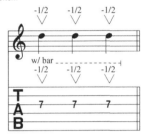

Additional Musical Definitions

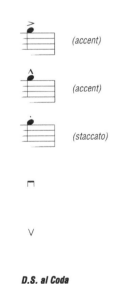

(accent)	•	Accentuate note (play it louder)
(accent)	•	Accentuate note with great intensity
(staccato)	•	Play the note short
	•	Downstroke
∨	•	Upstroke

D.S. al Coda
• Go back to the sign (𝄋), then play until the measure marked "**To Coda**," then skip to the section labelled "**Coda**."

D.S. al Fine
• Go back to the beginning of the song and play until the measure marked "**Fine**" (end).

Rhy. Fig.
• Label used to recall a recurring accompaniment pattern (usually chordal).

Riff
• Label used to recall composed, melodic lines (usually single notes) which recur.

Fill
• Label used to identify a brief melodic figure which is to be inserted into the arrangement.

Rhy. Fill
• A chordal version of a Fill.

tacet
• Instrument is silent (drops out).

• Repeat measures between signs.

• When a repeated section has different endings, play the first ending only the first time and the second ending only the second time.

NOTE: Tablature numbers in parentheses mean:
1. The note is being sustained over a system (note in standard notation is tied), or
2. The note is sustained, but a new articulation (such as a hammer-on, pull-off, slide or vibrato begins, or
3. The note is a barely audible "ghost" note (note in standard notation is also in parentheses).

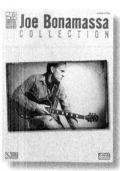
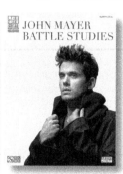